Table of Contents

1. Introduction to the Straight Line Technique
2. Understanding the Psychology of Cold Calling
3. Setting Clear Objectives for Cold Calls
4. Preparing Your Pitch: Research and Planning
5. Mastering the Opening: Hooking Your Prospect
6. Building Rapport and Establishing Trust
7. Handling Objections with Confidence
8. The Art of Qualifying Leads
9. Presenting Your Solution Effectively
10. Overcoming Common Challenges in Cold Calling
11. Closing the Deal: Using the Straight Line Technique
12. Follow-Up Strategies for Continued Engagement
13. Leveraging Technology in Cold Calling
14. Advanced Techniques for Experienced Cold Callers
15. The Importance of Persistence and Resilience
16. Measuring Success: Metrics and Analytics
17. Case Studies: Real-Life Examples of Cold Call Conversions
18. Conclusion: Mastering Cold Calling for Lasting Sales Success

Chapter 1: Introduction to the Straight Line Technique

Cold calling is often perceived as one of the most daunting tasks in sales.

It requires reaching out to prospects who may have never heard of your company or have little interest in your offerings.

However, with the right approach and technique, cold calling can be transformed into a powerful tool for generating leads and closing sales. Enter the Straight Line Technique.

What is the Straight Line Technique?

The Straight Line Technique, developed by Jordan Belfort, the "Wolf of Wall Street," is a systematic approach to cold calling that aims to streamline the sales process and guide prospects from initial contact to closing the deal along a straight line.

At its core, the Straight Line Technique is about maintaining control of the conversation, building rapport, handling objections, and ultimately, persuading prospects to take action.

Key Principles of the Straight Line Technique

> Control: In cold calling, maintaining control of the conversation is essential. The Straight Line Technique teaches sales professionals how to guide prospects along a predetermined path without veering off course or losing momentum.
>
> Certainty: Confidence is key in cold calling.
> The Straight Line Technique instils a sense of certainty in sales professionals, helping them project confidence, conviction, and enthusiasm to prospects.
>
> Connection: Building rapport and establishing a connection with prospects is critical in cold calling.
>
> The Straight Line Technique emphasises the importance of creating a genuine connection with prospects to earn their trust and cooperation.

Benefits of Using the Straight Line Technique

Efficiency: By following a structured approach, sales professionals can streamline the cold calling process, minimise wasted time and effort, and maximise their productivity.

Effectiveness: The Straight Line Technique is designed to increase conversion rates and drive results.
By guiding prospects along a predetermined path, sales professionals can overcome objections, address concerns, and close deals more effectively.

Empowerment: Mastering the Straight Line Technique empowers sales professionals to take control of their cold calling efforts, build confidence, and achieve their sales goals with greater consistency and success.

Getting Started with the Straight Line Technique

In the chapters ahead, we'll delve deeper into the principles, strategies, and best practices of the Straight Line Technique, providing actionable insights, practical tips, and real-world examples to help you excel in cold calling and turn prospects into customers along a straight line.

Chapter 2: Understanding the Psychology of Cold Calling

Cold calling can be intimidating, but understanding the psychology behind it can make all the difference in how successful you are at turning prospects into customers.

In this chapter, we'll explore the psychological principles that drive human behaviour during cold calls and how you can leverage them to your advantage.

The Power of Persuasion

At its core, cold calling is a form of persuasion.

It's about convincing someone to take action—whether it's scheduling a meeting, requesting more information, or making a purchase—based on a brief conversation over the phone.

To be effective at cold calling, you need to understand the principles of persuasion and how to apply them in your interactions with prospects.

Reciprocity

One of the most powerful principles of persuasion is reciprocity.

People have a natural tendency to want to reciprocate when someone does something for them.

In the context of cold calling, this means offering something of value to the prospect before asking for anything in return.

It could be a helpful tip, a valuable piece of information, or even just a friendly conversation.

By giving first, you increase the likelihood that the prospect will be receptive to your message and more willing to engage with you.

Social Proof

Another important principle of persuasion is social proof.

People are more likely to take action when they see others doing the same thing.

In the context of cold calling, this means providing evidence that others have found value in your product or service.

It could be testimonials from satisfied customers, case studies of successful implementations, or even just mentioning the names of well-known companies that are using your product.

By demonstrating that others have benefited from what you have to offer, you can increase the prospect's confidence in your solution and make them more likely to buy.

Authority

People are also more likely to be influenced by someone they perceive as an authority figure.

In the context of cold calling, this means positioning yourself as an expert in your field.

You can do this by demonstrating your knowledge and expertise during the conversation, citing relevant statistics or research, or mentioning any certifications or awards you've received.

By establishing yourself as an authority, you can increase the prospect's trust in you and make them more receptive to your message.

Overcoming Resistance and Objections

Even with a solid understanding of the principles of persuasion, you're likely to encounter resistance and objections during cold calls.

It's important to be prepared for these challenges and know how to respond effectively.

Here are some common objections you might encounter and strategies for overcoming them:

"I'm not interested."

This is perhaps the most common objection you'll hear during cold calls. The key to overcoming it is to acknowledge the prospect's response, but then pivot the conversation to focus on the value you can provide.

You might say something like, "I understand you may not be interested right now, but can I share with you how our solution has helped other companies in your industry?"

"I don't have time."

This objection is often a polite way of saying "no."

To overcome it, you can emphasise the brevity of your call and the value of the information you have to share.

You might say something like, "I'll be brief, but I believe I have something that could be of interest to you. Can I have just a minute of your time to explain?"

"I'm happy with my current provider."

This objection indicates that the prospect may not see a need for your solution.

To overcome it, you can highlight the unique value proposition of your product or service and how it differs from what they're currently using.

You might say something like, "I'm glad to hear you're satisfied with your current provider.

Our solution offers some unique features that could help you achieve even better results. Would you be open to learning more?"

Applying Psychological Principles in Your Cold Calls

Now that you understand the psychology behind cold calling and how to overcome resistance and objections, it's time to put these principles into action.

Here are some tips for applying psychological principles in your cold calls:

> Build rapport: Take the time to establish a connection with the prospect before diving into your pitch.
> Ask about their day, show genuine interest in their business, and find common ground to build rapport.
>
> Listen actively: Pay close attention to what the prospect is saying, and ask probing questions to uncover their needs, concerns, and objectives. The more

you understand about their situation, the better equipped you'll be to tailor your pitch to their specific needs.

Use persuasive language: Incorporate persuasive language and techniques into your conversation to increase the prospect's receptivity to your message.

This could include using social proof, authority, and reciprocity to bolster your credibility and influence.

Conclusion

Understanding the psychology of cold calling is essential for success in sales.

By leveraging principles of persuasion, overcoming resistance and objections, and applying psychological techniques in your cold calls, you can increase your effectiveness and achieve better results.

In the chapters ahead, we'll dive deeper into specific strategies and tactics for mastering the art of cold calling using the Straight Line Technique.

Chapter 3: Setting Clear Objectives for Cold Calls

Setting clear objectives is crucial for success in any endeavour, and cold calling is no exception.

In this chapter, we'll explore the importance of defining clear objectives for your cold calls, how to set SMART goals, and strategies for aligning your objectives with the Straight Line Technique.

The Importance of Setting Objectives

Before picking up the phone to make a cold call, it's essential to have a clear understanding of what you hope to accomplish.

Setting objectives helps you stay focused, motivated, and accountable throughout the cold calling process.

Here are some reasons why setting objectives is important:

Clarity: Objectives provide clarity and direction, helping you understand exactly what you're trying to achieve with each cold call.

Motivation: Clear objectives serve as motivation to keep pushing forward, even when faced with rejection or challenges during cold calls.

Accountability: Having defined objectives allows you to hold yourself accountable for your performance and track your progress over time.

Setting SMART Goals

When setting objectives for your cold calls, it's essential to make sure they are SMART: Specific, Measurable, Achievable, Relevant, and Time-bound.

Here's how to apply the SMART criteria to your cold calling objectives:

Specific: Your objectives should be clear, concise, and specific. Instead of setting a vague goal like "make more sales," specify exactly what you want to achieve with each cold call, such as "schedule a demo" or "secure a follow-up meeting."

Measurable: Your objectives should be measurable so that you can track your progress and evaluate your success.
Define specific metrics or criteria for success, such as the number of appointments booked or the percentage of leads converted.

Achievable: Your objectives should be realistic and achievable given your resources, skills, and circumstances.
Set goals that stretch you out of your comfort zone but are still within reach with effort and commitment.

Relevant: Your objectives should be aligned with your overall sales goals and objectives.
Ensure that each cold calling objective contributes to the larger goals of your sales strategy and supports your organisation's mission and vision.

Time-bound: Your objectives should have a clear timeframe or deadline for completion.
Set specific deadlines for achieving each objective, whether it's by the end of the day, week, or month, to create a sense of urgency and focus.

Strategies for Aligning Objectives with the Straight Line Technique

Once you've set SMART objectives for your cold calls, it's essential to align them with the principles of the Straight Line Technique.

Here are some strategies for doing so:

Focus on the next step: Instead of trying to close the deal on the first cold call, focus on moving the prospect along the straight line toward the next step in the sales process.

Whether it's scheduling a follow-up call, sending more information, or arranging a demo, aim to achieve a specific, tangible outcome with each cold call.

Qualify leads effectively: Use the Straight Line Technique to qualify leads quickly and efficiently during cold calls.
Ask targeted questions to assess the prospect's needs, budget, timeline, and decision-making authority, and determine whether they are a good fit for your offering before investing too much time and effort.

Handle objections proactively: Anticipate and address objections before they arise by incorporating them into your cold calling script and preparing effective responses in advance.
Use the Straight Line Technique to handle objections confidently and keep the conversation moving forward toward your objectives.

Create urgency: Use persuasive language and techniques to create a sense of urgency and compel prospects to take action during cold calls.

Whether it's highlighting limited-time offers, special promotions, or exclusive benefits, use the Straight Line Technique to motivate prospects to act now rather than later.

Conclusion

Setting clear objectives is essential for success in cold calling.

By defining SMART goals, aligning them with the principles of the Straight Line Technique, and implementing effective strategies for achieving them, you can increase your effectiveness, productivity, and results.

In the chapters ahead, we'll delve deeper into specific tactics and techniques for mastering cold calling and achieving your sales objectives.

Chapter 4: Preparing Your Pitch: Research and Planning

Effective cold calling requires meticulous preparation and strategic planning.

In this chapter, we'll delve deep into the essential steps of researching your prospects and crafting a compelling pitch that aligns with the Straight Line Technique.

The Significance of Thorough Research

Before initiating any cold call, investing time in comprehensive research is indispensable.

This preparatory step not only equips you with the necessary information about your prospect but also demonstrates your commitment and professionalism.

Here's why research is paramount in cold calling:

> Personalization: Tailoring your pitch to address the prospect's specific pain points and needs is key to capturing their interest.
> Research allows you to gather insights that enable personalised communication, making your pitch more relevant and compelling.

> Credibility: Demonstrating a profound understanding of the prospect's business and industry enhances your credibility and trustworthiness. It establishes you as a knowledgeable resource capable of providing valuable solutions.

Relevance: A well-researched cold call enables you to speak the prospect's language, addressing challenges and opportunities that are pertinent to their situation.

This relevance increases the likelihood of engagement and receptivity to your message.

Strategies for Gathering Information

To conduct effective research for your cold calls, it's essential to employ a variety of strategies and utilise diverse sources of information.

Here are some proven methods:

Company Website: Start by thoroughly exploring the prospect's website to gain insights into their products, services, target market, company culture, and recent news or announcements.

Social Media: Investigate the prospect's social media profiles, including LinkedIn, Twitter, and Facebook, to learn more about their professional background, interests, and recent activities.

Pay attention to any posts or updates that provide valuable context for your conversation.

Online Databases: Leverage online databases and business directories to gather additional information about the prospect's company, such as industry rankings, financial performance, key personnel, and contact details.

Industry Publications: Stay informed about industry trends, challenges, and best practices by reading relevant publications, blogs, forums, and news sites.

Look for insights that can help you position your offering as a valuable solution to the prospect's challenges.

Structuring Your Pitch for Maximum Impact

Crafting a compelling pitch is essential for capturing and maintaining the prospect's interest during a cold call.

The structure of your pitch should be designed to guide the prospect along the straight line toward the desired outcome.

Here's how to structure your pitch effectively:

> Introduction: Start with a brief introduction that includes your name, company, and purpose for calling.
> Quickly transition to a hook—a compelling reason for the prospect to continue the conversation based on your research and insights.
>
> Rapport-Building: Establish rapport with the prospect by demonstrating genuine interest in their business and asking open-ended questions to encourage dialogue.
> Listen actively to their responses and look for opportunities to connect on a personal or professional level.
>
> Value Proposition: Clearly articulate the value proposition of your product or service, focusing on how it addresses the prospect's specific needs, challenges, or objectives.
> Highlight key benefits and unique selling points that differentiate your offering from competitors and resonate with the prospect.
>
> Call to Action: Close your pitch with a clear call to action—a specific, tangible next step that you want the prospect to take.
> Whether it's scheduling a follow-up call, requesting a meeting, or downloading a whitepaper, make it easy for the prospect to say yes and move forward in the sales process.

Incorporating the Straight Line Technique

Throughout the research and planning process, it's essential to keep the principles of the Straight Line Technique in mind.

Here's how to incorporate the Straight Line Technique into your cold call preparation:

> Maintain Control: Use your research to guide the conversation and maintain control of the interaction, steering the prospect along the straight line toward the desired outcome.
>
> Build Certainty: Demonstrate confidence and conviction in your pitch, drawing on your knowledge and expertise to instil certainty in the prospect and increase their confidence in your solution.
>
> Establish Rapport: Use your research to find common ground and establish rapport with the prospect, showing that you understand their business and care about their success.

Conclusion

Thorough research and strategic planning are essential prerequisites for effective cold calling.

By investing time in gathering relevant information about your prospects and crafting a compelling pitch that aligns with the Straight Line Technique, you can increase your chances of success and achieve better results in your cold calling efforts.

In the following chapters, we'll explore specific strategies and techniques for mastering each stage of the cold calling process.

Chapter 5: Mastering the Opening: Hooking Your Prospect

The opening of a cold call is your gateway to engage with your prospect effectively.

It's your chance to make a memorable impression, capture their interest, and pave the way for a meaningful conversation.

In this chapter, we'll explore in-depth strategies for crafting a compelling opening that hooks your prospect's attention and keeps them engaged throughout the call.

Understanding the Significance of the Opening

The opening moments of a cold call are crucial because they set the tone for the entire interaction.

It's your opportunity to make a positive impression, establish rapport, and build credibility with the prospect.

A strong opening can captivate the prospect's attention and make them receptive to your message, while a weak or uninspiring one can lead to a quick dismissal.

Here's why mastering the opening is vital:

> First Impressions: The opening of a cold call creates the prospect's initial impression of you and your company.
> A compelling opening can leave a positive impact and lay the foundation for a productive conversation.

Engagement: A well-crafted opening captures the prospect's attention and keeps them engaged throughout the call.
It hooks their interest and makes them eager to learn more about what you have to offer.

Curiosity: An effective opening generates curiosity and intrigue, prompting the prospect to want to hear more.
It creates a sense of anticipation and excitement about what you're going to say next.

Strategies for Crafting a Compelling Opening

Crafting a compelling opening requires careful planning and strategic execution.

It should be concise, relevant, and tailored to the prospect's needs and interests.

Here are some strategies for crafting a compelling opening that hooks your prospect's attention:

Start with a Hook: Begin your cold call with a hook—a compelling reason for the prospect to continue the conversation.
This could be a relevant insight, a thought-provoking question, or a personalised observation based on your research.
The key is to grab their attention and make them curious to hear more.

Focus on the Prospect: Make the opening of your cold call all about the prospect.
Show genuine interest in their business, industry, and challenges. Ask open-ended questions to encourage dialogue and demonstrate that you understand their needs and concerns.
This approach builds rapport and establishes a connection with the prospect from the outset.

Highlight Benefits: Clearly articulate the benefits of your product or service early in the conversation.
Focus on how it addresses the prospect's specific pain points and solves their problems.
Highlight key benefits and unique selling points that resonate with the prospect and differentiate your offering from competitors.
This helps the prospect see the value in continuing the conversation.

Create Curiosity: Use your opening to create curiosity and intrigue about what you have to offer.
Tease the prospect with a tantalising glimpse of the value you can provide, and leave them wanting to hear more. By sparking their curiosity, you increase their motivation to engage with you further and learn about your solution.

Examples of Compelling Openings

Let's delve into some examples of compelling openings for cold calls:

Insight-Based Opening: "Hello [Prospect's Name], I recently came across your company's latest blog post on [topic].
It got me thinking about how our solution could help you capitalise on the trends you discussed.
I'd love to share some ideas with you.
Would you be open to a brief conversation?"

Question-Based Opening: "Hi [Prospect's Name], I noticed that your company is expanding into [new market]. What challenges are you encountering as you navigate this growth?
Our solution has helped similar companies overcome similar obstacles, and I believe it could be beneficial for you as well. Can we discuss further?"

Personalised Opening: "Good morning [Prospect's Name], I read your recent interview in [publication], and I was impressed by your insights on [topic]. It got me thinking about how our solution aligns with your goals.
I'd love to explore this further with you. Are you available for a brief conversation?"

Overcoming Common Challenges in the Opening

Despite your best efforts, you may encounter challenges when crafting your opening. Here are some common challenges and strategies for overcoming them:

Gatekeepers: If you encounter a gatekeeper, such as a receptionist or assistant, remain polite and professional.
Clearly state your purpose for calling and request to speak directly with the decision-maker.

Provide a brief overview of why your call is relevant and why it's essential to connect with the prospect.

Short Attention Spans: In today's fast-paced world, people have short attention spans.
To keep your prospect engaged, keep your opening concise and to the point. Focus on the most compelling aspects of your offer and avoid lengthy explanations or unnecessary details.

Rejection: Rejection is a natural part of cold calling.
If the prospect is not interested or dismisses your call, remain courteous and professional. Thank them for their time and move on to the next call without dwelling on the rejection.
Remember that each call is an opportunity to learn and improve.

Conclusion

Mastering the opening of a cold call is essential for capturing the prospect's attention, establishing rapport, and setting the stage for a productive conversation.

By crafting a compelling opening that hooks the prospect's attention and keeps them engaged, you can increase your chances of success and achieve better results in your cold calling efforts.

In the following chapters, we'll explore specific strategies and techniques for mastering each stage of the cold calling process.

Chapter 6: Building Rapport and Establishing Trust

Building rapport and establishing trust are fundamental aspects of successful cold calling.

In this chapter, we'll delve deep into the importance of rapport-building, strategies for creating a genuine connection with your prospects, and techniques for earning their trust using the Straight Line Technique.

The Significance of Rapport and Trust in Cold Calling

Rapport and trust are the foundation of any successful relationship, including those formed through cold calling.

Establishing a strong rapport and building trust with your prospects lays the groundwork for meaningful conversations, fosters open communication, and increases the likelihood of securing a positive outcome.

Here's why rapport-building and trust-building are crucial in cold calling:

> Open Communication: A strong rapport creates an environment of open communication, where prospects feel comfortable sharing their needs, concerns, and objectives with you.
> This enables you to gain valuable insights and tailor your approach to meet their specific needs effectively.
>
> Positive Perception: Building rapport and trust enhances the prospect's perception of you and your company.
> When prospects feel valued, respected, and understood, they are more likely to view you as a trusted advisor rather than a pushy salesperson.
>
> Increased Engagement: Establishing trust and rapport increases the prospect's engagement and receptivity to your message.
> They are more likely to listen attentively, ask questions, and consider your offer seriously when they feel a connection with you.

Strategies for Building Rapport

Building rapport with your prospects requires genuine effort, empathy, and effective communication skills.

Here are some strategies for creating a genuine connection and building rapport during cold calls:

> Active Listening: Practise active listening by giving your full attention to the prospect, acknowledging their statements, and responding thoughtfully. Show genuine interest in what they have to say and ask follow-up questions to demonstrate your understanding.
>
> Empathy: Put yourself in the prospect's shoes and empathise with their challenges, concerns, and objectives. Show empathy by acknowledging their feelings and validating their experiences.

This helps create a sense of trust and understanding between you and the prospect.

Authenticity: Be authentic and genuine in your interactions with prospects. Avoid using canned scripts or salesy language that may come across as insincere.
Instead, be yourself, speak from the heart, and let your personality shine through.

Common Ground: Look for common ground and shared interests that you can bond over with the prospect.
Whether it's a mutual connection, a shared hobby, or a similar experience, finding common ground helps establish rapport and build a sense of camaraderie.

Techniques for Establishing Trust

Establishing trust with your prospects is essential for gaining their confidence and credibility.

Here are some techniques for earning trust using the Straight Line Technique:

Transparency: Be transparent and honest in your interactions with prospects. Avoid exaggerating or making unrealistic promises that you can't deliver on. Instead, be upfront about what you can offer and how it can benefit the prospect.

Social Proof: Use social proof to build trust with prospects by highlighting testimonials, case studies, or success stories from satisfied customers. Sharing real-life examples of how your product or service has helped others builds credibility and demonstrates value.

Authority: Position yourself as an authority in your field by sharing relevant expertise, insights, and industry knowledge with prospects.
Show that you understand their challenges and can provide valuable solutions based on your expertise and experience.

Consistency: Be consistent in your messaging and actions to build trust over time.
Follow through on your commitments, deliver on your promises, and provide exceptional service to every prospect you interact with.
Consistency breeds trust and reliability.

Overcoming Common Challenges in Rapport-Building

Despite your best efforts, you may encounter challenges when building rapport with prospects.

Here are some common challenges and strategies for overcoming them:

> Resistance: If a prospect seems hesitant or resistant to building rapport, be patient and persistent.
> Continue to engage them in conversation, ask open-ended questions, and look for opportunities to connect on a personal level.
>
> Time Constraints: In today's fast-paced world, prospects may have limited time to spare for cold calls.
> Respect their time by keeping your interactions brief and focused. Get to the point quickly, but also take the time to establish rapport and build trust before moving on to your pitch.
>
> Cultural Differences: When cold calling prospects from diverse backgrounds or cultures, be mindful of cultural differences in communication styles and social norms.
> Adapt your approach accordingly and show respect for the prospect's cultural preferences and customs.

Conclusion

Building rapport and establishing trust are essential components of successful cold calling.

By practising active listening, empathy, authenticity, and utilising techniques like transparency, social proof, authority, and consistency, you can create genuine connections with your prospects and earn their trust.

In the following chapters, we'll explore specific strategies and techniques for mastering each stage of the cold calling process.

Chapter 7: Handling Objections with Confidence

Objections are a natural part of the sales process, especially in cold calling.

In this chapter, we'll explore the common objections you may encounter during cold calls, strategies for handling them with confidence, and techniques for turning objections into opportunities using the Straight Line Technique.

Understanding Common Objections in Cold Calling

Objections are expressions of resistance or concerns that prospects raise during a sales conversation.

In cold calling, objections can arise due to various reasons, such as scepticism about the product or service, budget constraints, or lack of trust in the salesperson.

Here are some common objections you may encounter:

> Price Objections: Prospects may object to the price of your product or service, stating that it's too expensive or not within their budget.
>
> Timing Objections: Prospects may express concerns about the timing of your offer, indicating that they're not ready to make a decision or take action at the moment.
>
> Need Objections: Prospects may question the need for your product or service, stating that they're satisfied with their current solution or don't see the value in what you're offering.
>
> Authority Objections: Prospects may raise objections related to their authority to make purchasing decisions, stating that they need to consult with other stakeholders or obtain approval from higher-ups.

Competitor Objections: Prospects may compare your offering to that of competitors and raise objections based on perceived differences or advantages of competing solutions.

Strategies for Handling Objections

Handling objections effectively requires preparation, empathy, and confidence.

Here are some strategies for handling objections with confidence during cold calls:

Listen Actively: Practise active listening when prospects raise objections, acknowledging their concerns and giving them space to express themselves fully.

Empathise: Show empathy and understanding when addressing objections, acknowledging the prospect's perspective and validating their concerns.

Clarify: Ask clarifying questions to gain a deeper understanding of the prospect's objections and the underlying reasons behind them.

Provide Solutions: Offer solutions or alternatives to address the prospect's objections, focusing on how your product or service can meet their needs and overcome their challenges.

Highlight Benefits: Reinforce the benefits and value of your offering when responding to objections, emphasising how it can help the prospect achieve their goals and solve their problems.

Use Social Proof: Share testimonials, case studies, or success stories from satisfied customers to alleviate concerns and build credibility.

Techniques for Turning Objections into Opportunities

Instead of viewing objections as roadblocks, see them as opportunities to engage with the prospect, address their concerns, and move the conversation forward.

Here are some techniques for turning objections into opportunities using the Straight Line Technique:

> Acknowledge and Pivot: Acknowledge the prospect's objection, then pivot the conversation back to the benefits and value of your offering.
> Redirect their focus away from the objection and towards the solution.
>
> Reframe the Objection: Reframe the prospect's objection as an opportunity by highlighting how addressing it can benefit them.
> Turn their objection into a discussion about how your product or service can solve their problem or meet their needs.
>
> Ask Permission to Proceed: Ask the prospect for permission to address their objection and continue the conversation.
> This demonstrates respect for their concerns and gives them a sense of control over the interaction.
>
> Offer a Trial or Demo: Offer to provide a trial or demo of your product or service to address the prospect's concerns and demonstrate its value firsthand.
>
> Follow Up: If the prospect's objection cannot be resolved immediately, offer to follow up with additional information or resources to address their concerns.

Overcoming Common Challenges in Handling Objections

While handling objections, you may encounter various challenges that require patience and skill to overcome.

Here are some common challenges and strategies for addressing them:

> Lack of Information: If you're unable to address the prospect's objection due to a lack of information, be honest and transparent about it.
> Offer to follow up with the necessary details or resources to address their concerns adequately.
> Resistance: If the prospect is resistant to addressing their objection, take a step back and empathise with their perspective.

Try to understand the root cause of their resistance and address it sensitively.

Rejection: If the prospect rejects your attempts to address their objection, remain polite and professional.
Thank them for their feedback and offer to stay in touch for future opportunities.

Conclusion

Handling objections with confidence is a crucial skill in cold calling.

By listening actively, empathising with the prospect, providing solutions, and turning objections into opportunities using the Straight Line Technique, you can navigate objections effectively and move closer to closing the sale.

In the following chapters, we'll explore specific strategies and techniques for mastering each stage of the cold calling process.

Chapter 8: The Art of Qualifying Leads

Qualifying leads is an essential step in the cold calling process that ensures you're focusing your time and efforts on prospects who are most likely to become customers.

In this chapter, we'll explore the importance of lead qualification, strategies for effectively qualifying leads, and techniques for maximising your success rate using the Straight Line Technique.

The Importance of Lead Qualification

Lead qualification is the process of determining whether a prospect meets the criteria for being a viable sales opportunity.

It involves evaluating various factors, such as the prospect's needs, budget, authority, timeline, and fit with your product or service.

Qualifying leads is crucial for several reasons:

Time Efficiency: Qualifying leads helps you prioritise your time and resources by focusing on prospects who are most likely to convert into customers.

This maximises your efficiency and allows you to allocate your efforts where they'll have the greatest impact.

Improved Conversion Rates: By qualifying leads effectively, you can identify high-quality prospects who have a genuine need for your product or service and are more likely to make a purchase.
This leads to higher conversion rates and increased sales success.

Better Targeting: Qualifying leads enables you to tailor your approach and messaging to the specific needs and preferences of each prospect.
This improves the relevance and effectiveness of your sales pitch, making it more compelling and persuasive.

Enhanced Customer Satisfaction: By focusing on qualified leads, you can ensure that you're offering solutions that align with the prospect's needs and objectives.
This leads to higher levels of customer satisfaction and loyalty in the long run.

Strategies for Effective Lead Qualification

Effective lead qualification requires a systematic approach and careful consideration of various factors.

Here are some strategies for effectively qualifying leads during cold calls:

Define Ideal Customer Profiles: Start by defining your ideal customer profiles based on demographic, firmographic, and psychographic criteria.
Identify characteristics that indicate a good fit with your product or service, such as industry, company size, budget, pain points, and buying behaviour.

Ask Qualifying Questions: During cold calls, ask probing questions to gather information and assess the prospect's needs, challenges, and objectives.

Use open-ended questions to encourage dialogue and uncover valuable insights that can help you qualify the lead effectively.

Listen for Buying Signals: Pay attention to verbal and non-verbal cues that indicate the prospect's level of interest and readiness to buy.
Look for buying signals such as asking detailed questions, expressing enthusiasm, or indicating a willingness to explore your offer further.

Evaluate Fit and Budget: Assess whether the prospect's needs align with your product or service and whether they have the budget and authority to make a purchase decision.
Determine whether the prospect meets your qualification criteria and whether pursuing the opportunity is worth your time and resources.

Techniques for Maximising Success with Qualified Leads

Once you've identified qualified leads, it's essential to maximise your success rate by effectively engaging and converting them into customers.

Here are some techniques for maximising success with qualified leads using the Straight Line Technique:

Customise Your Pitch: Tailor your sales pitch to address the specific needs, challenges, and objectives of each qualified lead.
Highlight how your product or service can solve their problems and deliver value that aligns with their goals.

Leverage Social Proof: Use testimonials, case studies, or success stories from satisfied customers to build credibility and demonstrate the effectiveness of your solution.
Share real-life examples of how your product or service has helped similar companies achieve their objectives.

Create a Sense of Urgency: Create a sense of urgency by highlighting time-sensitive benefits or limited-time offers that encourage qualified leads to take action quickly.
Emphasise the consequences of inaction and the benefits of acting now to motivate prospects to move forward.

Handle Objections Proactively: Anticipate and address potential objections that qualified leads may raise during the sales process.

Prepare persuasive responses and solutions to overcome objections and reassure prospects about the value and benefits of your offer.

Overcoming Common Challenges in Lead Qualification

While qualifying leads, you may encounter various challenges that require patience and skill to overcome.

Here are some common challenges and strategies for addressing them:

Limited Information: If you have limited information about the prospect, use research tools and techniques to gather additional insights and qualify the lead more effectively.

Look for publicly available information, such as company websites, social media profiles, and industry reports, to supplement your understanding.

Scepticism: If the prospect is sceptical or guarded during the qualification process, focus on building rapport and establishing trust by demonstrating empathy, credibility, and authenticity.
Address their concerns openly and transparently, and provide evidence to support your claims.

Budget Constraints: If the prospect expresses concerns about budget constraints, explore flexible pricing options or value-added services that align with their budgetary requirements.
Highlight the return on investment (ROI) and long-term benefits of your solution to justify the investment.

Conclusion

Effective lead qualification is essential for maximising your success in cold calling.

By defining ideal customer profiles, asking qualifying questions, listening for buying signals, and evaluating fit and budget, you can identify high-quality prospects who are most likely to become customers.

By leveraging the Straight Line Technique to engage and convert qualified leads, you can increase your conversion rates and achieve better results in your cold calling efforts.

Chapter 9: Presenting Your Solution Effectively

Presenting your solution effectively is a critical step in the cold calling process.

It's your opportunity to showcase the value of your product or service, address the prospect's needs and concerns, and persuade them to take action.

In this chapter, we'll explore the key components of an effective solution presentation, strategies for delivering your pitch with impact, and techniques for maximising your persuasive power using the Straight Line Technique.

Understanding the Objectives of Your Solution Presentation

The primary objectives of your solution presentation are to educate the prospect about your product or service, demonstrate its value and benefits, and convince them to take the next steps in the sales process.

Your presentation should be informative, engaging, and persuasive, with a focus on addressing the prospect's specific needs and challenges.

Here are the key objectives of your solution presentation:

> Educate: Provide the prospect with a clear understanding of how your product or service works, what it can do, and how it can benefit them.
> Explain key features, functionalities, and use cases in a way that resonates with their needs and objectives.
>
> Engage: Capture the prospect's attention and maintain their interest throughout the presentation by delivering content that is relevant, compelling, and tailored to their interests.

Use visuals, stories, and real-life examples to bring your solution to life and make it memorable.

Persuade: Persuade the prospect to take action by highlighting the unique value proposition of your solution and addressing any objections or concerns they may have.
Use persuasive language, testimonials, and social proof to build credibility and trust.

Key Components of an Effective Solution Presentation

An effective solution presentation should include several key components that address the prospect's needs, demonstrate the value of your offering, and guide them towards a positive decision.

Here are the essential components of an effective solution presentation:

Introduction: Start by introducing yourself, your company, and the purpose of the presentation.
Set the stage for what the prospect can expect to learn and gain from the presentation.

Needs Analysis: Review the prospect's needs, challenges, and objectives based on the information gathered during the qualification process.
Demonstrate your understanding of their pain points and show how your solution can address them effectively.

Product Demonstration: Showcase the features, functionalities, and benefits of your product or service through a live demonstration or presentation.
Highlight key capabilities and use cases that are relevant to the prospect's needs and objectives.

Value Proposition: Clearly articulate the unique value proposition of your solution and how it differentiates you from competitors.
Emphasise the benefits and outcomes that the prospect can expect to achieve by using your product or service.

Case Studies/Testimonials: Share real-life examples of how your solution has helped other customers achieve their goals and solve similar problems.

Use case studies, testimonials, or success stories to provide social proof and build credibility.

ROI/Value Analysis: Quantify the return on investment (ROI) or value proposition of your solution by demonstrating the potential cost savings, revenue growth, or other tangible benefits that the prospect can expect to realise.

Next Steps: Conclude the presentation by outlining the next steps in the sales process and inviting the prospect to take action.
Provide clear instructions on how they can move forward, such as scheduling a follow-up meeting, requesting a proposal, or signing up for a trial.

Strategies for Delivering Your Pitch with Impact

Delivering your pitch with impact requires careful preparation, confident delivery, and effective communication skills.

Here are some strategies for delivering your solution presentation with impact:

Know Your Audience: Tailor your presentation to the needs, preferences, and interests of your audience.
Research the prospect's industry, company, and role to customise your messaging and make it relevant to their situation.

Practise Active Listening: Listen attentively to the prospect's feedback and questions during the presentation, and respond thoughtfully to address their concerns and keep them engaged.

Use Visual Aids: Use visual aids such as slides, charts, and graphs to enhance your presentation and make complex concepts easier to understand.
Keep visuals clean, simple, and visually appealing to maximise their impact.

Tell Stories: Incorporate storytelling into your presentation to make it more engaging and memorable.
Use anecdotes, case studies, or personal experiences to illustrate key points and connect with the prospect on an emotional level.

Be Confident: Project confidence and enthusiasm throughout the presentation to inspire trust and credibility in your solution.

Maintain eye contact, speak clearly and assertively, and exude passion for what you're presenting.

Handle Objections Gracefully: Anticipate potential objections that may arise during the presentation and prepare persuasive responses in advance. Address objections calmly and confidently, and use them as opportunities to reinforce the value of your solution.

Techniques for Maximising Persuasive Power

To maximise your persuasive power during the solution presentation, leverage the principles of influence and persuasion outlined in the Straight Line Technique. Here are some techniques to consider:

Reciprocity: Offer something of value to the prospect, such as a free trial, sample, or consultation, to create a sense of reciprocity and increase their willingness to reciprocate by taking action.

Social Proof: Highlight testimonials, case studies, or success stories from satisfied customers to provide social proof and build credibility.
Use peer references and endorsements to reassure the prospect about the effectiveness of your solution.

Scarcity: Create a sense of urgency by emphasising limited-time offers, exclusive deals, or scarcity of inventory.
Encourage the prospect to act quickly to take advantage of the opportunity before it's gone.

Authority: Position yourself as an authority in your field by sharing relevant expertise, insights, and industry knowledge.
Demonstrate your credibility and expertise to build trust and confidence in your solution.

Consistency: Emphasise the alignment between the prospect's needs and objectives and the benefits of your solution.

Highlight how choosing your product or service is consistent with their goals and values.

Overcoming Common Challenges in Solution Presentations

While delivering your solution presentation, you may encounter various challenges that require patience, adaptability, and skill to overcome.

Here are some common challenges and strategies for addressing them:

Technical Issues: If you experience technical difficulties during the presentation, remain calm and composed.
Have backup plans in place, such as printed materials or alternative presentation formats, to ensure a smooth delivery.

Lack of Engagement: If the prospect seems disengaged or distracted during the presentation, try to re-engage them by asking questions, soliciting feedback, or introducing interactive elements.
Keep the presentation dynamic and interactive to maintain the prospect's interest.

Information Overload: Avoid overwhelming the prospect with too much information or technical jargon.
Keep the presentation focused on the most relevant and compelling aspects of your solution, and be prepared to provide additional details or clarification as needed.

Conclusion

Presenting your solution effectively is a critical step in the cold calling process. By understanding the objectives of your presentation, incorporating key components, delivering your pitch with impact, and maximising your persuasive power, you can increase your chances of success and achieve better results in your cold calling efforts.

In the following chapters, we'll explore specific strategies and techniques for mastering each stage of the cold calling process.

Chapter 10: Overcoming Common Challenges in Cold Calling

Cold calling is a dynamic and challenging endeavour that requires resilience, adaptability, and perseverance.

In this chapter, we'll explore the common challenges that cold callers face and provide strategies for overcoming them effectively to achieve success using the Straight Line Technique.

Understanding Common Challenges in Cold Calling

Cold calling presents a unique set of challenges that can hinder your effectiveness and impact your success rate.

Understanding these challenges is the first step towards overcoming them. Here are some common challenges in cold calling:

> Rejection: Facing rejection is an inherent part of cold calling. Prospects may hang up on you, express disinterest, or outright reject your offer, which can be demoralising and discouraging.
>
> Gatekeepers: Dealing with gatekeepers, such as receptionists or assistants, can be challenging as they often screen calls and prevent you from reaching decision-makers.
>
> Lack of Interest: Some prospects may simply not be interested in what you have to offer, making it difficult to capture their attention or engage them in a meaningful conversation.
>
> Objections: Overcoming objections from prospects can be challenging, especially if you're unprepared or unsure how to respond effectively.
>
> Time Constraints: Cold calling requires time and persistence, but time constraints can limit your ability to make a sufficient number of calls or follow up with prospects effectively.

Strategies for Overcoming Common Challenges

While cold calling presents its fair share of challenges, there are strategies you can employ to overcome them and improve your success rate.

Here are some effective strategies for overcoming common challenges in cold calling:

> Develop Resilience: Rejection is inevitable in cold calling, but it's essential to develop resilience and not take rejection personally.
> Treat each rejection as a learning opportunity and focus on the next call.
>
> Build Rapport: Establishing rapport with prospects can help overcome resistance and objections.
> Take the time to build rapport by asking open-ended questions, actively listening, and showing genuine interest in the prospect's needs.
>
> Navigate Gatekeepers: Develop strategies for bypassing gatekeepers and reaching decision-makers directly.
> Build rapport with gatekeepers, use creative tactics to get past them, or leverage social media and email to connect with prospects outside of traditional cold calling.
>
> Address Objections Proactively: Anticipate common objections and prepare persuasive responses in advance.
> Use the Straight Line Technique to address objections confidently and redirect the conversation back to the value of your offer.
>
> Qualify Leads Effectively: Focus your efforts on qualified leads who are more likely to convert into customers.
> Qualify leads based on their needs, budget, authority, and fit with your offering to maximise your success rate.
>
> Manage Time Wisely: Prioritise your time and resources by focusing on high-value activities and prospects.
> Allocate dedicated time blocks for cold calling, follow-up calls, and administrative tasks to ensure efficient use of your time.

Leveraging the Straight Line Technique to Overcome Challenges

The Straight Line Technique provides a structured framework for overcoming common challenges in cold calling and guiding prospects through the sales process effectively.

Here's how you can leverage the Straight Line Technique to overcome challenges:

> Engage: Use the opening phase of the Straight Line Technique to capture the prospect's attention and establish rapport quickly.
> Start with a strong hook and transition smoothly into the conversation to keep the prospect engaged.

> Qualify: Qualify prospects effectively using the qualification phase of the Straight Line Technique.
> Ask probing questions to uncover their needs, challenges, and objectives, and evaluate whether they're a good fit for your offering.

> Present: Present your solution confidently and persuasively using the presentation phase of the Straight Line Technique.
> Highlight the benefits and value of your offer, address objections proactively, and guide the prospect towards a positive decision.

> Close: Close the deal with confidence using the closing phase of the Straight Line Technique.
> Ask for the sale directly, overcome any remaining objections, and secure commitment from the prospect to move forward.

Case Studies: Real-Life Examples of Overcoming Challenges

To illustrate how the Straight Line Technique can help overcome common challenges in cold calling, let's explore two case studies:

Case Study 1: Overcoming Rejection

John, a sales representative, faced rejection from several prospects during his cold calling sessions.

Instead of becoming discouraged, he used the Straight Line Technique to refine his approach and address objections confidently.

By focusing on building rapport, qualifying leads effectively, and using persuasive closing techniques, John was able to overcome rejection and achieve success in his cold calling efforts.

Case Study 2: Navigating Gatekeepers

Sarah, a sales manager, encountered difficulties reaching decision-makers due to gatekeepers screening her calls.

She employed creative tactics, such as calling outside of typical business hours or using LinkedIn to connect with prospects directly.

By leveraging the Straight Line Technique to build rapport with gatekeepers and establish credibility with decision-makers, Sarah successfully navigated gatekeepers and secured meetings with key prospects.

Conclusion

Cold calling presents numerous challenges, from rejection and objections to time constraints and gatekeepers.

However, by employing effective strategies, leveraging the Straight Line Technique, and learning from real-life examples, you can overcome these challenges and achieve success in your cold calling efforts.

In the following chapters, we'll continue to explore advanced techniques and best practices for mastering the art of cold calling.

Chapter 11: Closing the Deal: Using the Straight Line Technique

Closing the deal is the culmination of the cold calling process, where you secure commitment from the prospect to move forward with your offer.

In this chapter, we'll delve into the art of closing the deal using the Straight Line Technique, exploring the key principles, strategies, and techniques for achieving success.

Understanding the Importance of Closing

Closing the deal is the ultimate goal of any sales interaction, including cold calling.

It's the moment when all your efforts and preparation pay off, and you successfully convert a prospect into a customer.

Closing is essential for several reasons:

> Revenue Generation: Closing deals directly contribute to revenue generation for your business, driving growth and profitability.

> Relationship Building: Successfully closing a deal establishes a foundation for a long-term relationship with the customer, leading to repeat business and referrals.

> Validation of Efforts: Closing a deal validates your sales efforts and demonstrates your effectiveness as a sales professional.

The Straight Line Technique for Closing

The Straight Line Technique provides a structured framework for guiding prospects through the closing process effectively.

It consists of four key phases: Engage, Qualify, Present, and Close.

Let's explore how each phase contributes to closing the deal:

> Engage: The Engage phase sets the stage for the closing process by capturing the prospect's attention and establishing rapport.
> It involves using a strong opening statement, building trust, and creating a positive impression.

> Qualify: In the Qualify phase, you gather information about the prospect's needs, challenges, and objectives to determine their suitability as a customer.

Qualifying leads effectively ensures that you're focusing your efforts on prospects who are most likely to convert into customers.

Present: The Present phase involves showcasing the value and benefits of your product or service to the prospect.
It's an opportunity to address their needs and concerns, demonstrate how your offering meets their
requirements, and differentiate yourself from competitors.

Close: The Close phase is where you ask for the sale directly and secure commitment from the prospect to move forward.
It involves overcoming objections, addressing any remaining concerns, and guiding the prospect towards a positive decision.

Strategies for Effective Closing

Closing the deal requires a combination of confidence, persuasion, and strategic thinking.

Here are some strategies for effectively closing deals using the Straight Line Technique:

Ask for the Sale: Be direct and ask for the sale confidently. Use clear, concise language and avoid beating around the bush.
For example, "Based on what we've discussed, are you ready to move forward with our offer today?"

Create a Sense of Urgency: Encourage the prospect to take action by creating a sense of urgency.
Highlight limited-time offers, exclusive deals, or deadlines to motivate them to make a decision.

Handle Objections Proactively: Anticipate objections that the prospect may raise and prepare persuasive responses in advance.
Address objections calmly and confidently, and use them as opportunities to reinforce the value of your offer.

Offer Incentives: Provide incentives or bonuses to sweeten the deal and incentivize the prospect to commit.
Offer discounts, extended trial periods, or additional features to make your offer more attractive.

Use Trial Closes: Throughout the conversation, use trial closes to gauge the prospect's readiness to buy.
Ask questions such as "If we could meet your requirements within your budget, would you be ready to move forward?"

Follow Up: If the prospect is not ready to commit immediately, offer to follow up with additional information or resources to address their concerns.
Set a specific timeline for follow-up and maintain regular communication to keep the momentum going.

Leveraging Advanced Techniques for Closing

In addition to the basic strategies outlined above, there are advanced techniques you can use to enhance your closing skills further.

These include:

Assumptive Close: Assume the sale by phrasing your questions and statements in a way that implies the prospect has already agreed to move forward.
For example, "When would you like to schedule delivery?"

Alternative Close: Present the prospect with two or more options, all of which lead to a positive outcome for you.
For example, "Would you prefer to start with our basic package or upgrade to the premium option?"

Puppy Dog Close: Offer the prospect a trial or demo of your product or service with no obligation to buy.
Once they experience the benefits firsthand, they'll be more likely to commit.

Silence Close: After presenting your offer, remain silent and wait for the prospect to respond.
Often, the discomfort of silence prompts them to make a decision or reveal their true objections.

Overcoming Common Challenges in Closing

Closing deals can be challenging, especially if you encounter resistance or objections from the prospect.

Here are some common challenges and strategies for overcoming them:

Fear of Rejection: Fear of rejection can prevent you from asking for the sale. Overcome this fear by reframing rejection as a natural part of the sales process and focusing on the value you can provide to the prospect.

Lack of Confidence: Confidence is key to effective closing.
Build your confidence by practising your pitch, mastering product knowledge, and role-playing different closing scenarios with colleagues or mentors.

Handling Objections: Objections are a natural part of the closing process. Address objections proactively by empathising with the prospect's concerns, providing relevant information, and offering solutions to overcome their objections.

Timing: Timing is crucial in closing deals. Avoid rushing the prospect or pushing them into a decision before they're ready.
Instead, listen attentively, gauge their readiness, and close at the appropriate moment.

Conclusion

Closing the deal is the final step in the cold calling process and requires skill, confidence, and strategic thinking.

By leveraging the Straight Line Technique, employing effective closing strategies, and overcoming common challenges, you can increase your success rate and achieve better results in your cold calling efforts.

In the following chapters, we'll continue to explore advanced techniques and best practices for mastering the art of cold calling.

Chapter 12: Follow-Up Strategies for Continued Engagement

Effective follow-up is essential for maintaining momentum, building rapport, and ultimately converting prospects into customers.

In this chapter, we'll explore the importance of follow-up in the cold calling process, strategies for crafting compelling follow-up messages, and techniques for staying top-of-mind with prospects using the Straight Line Technique.

The Importance of Follow-Up

Follow-up is a critical component of the sales process that allows you to nurture relationships, address concerns, and guide prospects towards a positive decision.

It demonstrates your commitment to providing value and support to the prospect and reinforces their confidence in your offering.

Here are some reasons why follow-up is important:

> Builds Rapport: Follow-up helps you build rapport and establish trust with prospects over time.
> By staying in touch and providing valuable information, you can strengthen your relationship and position yourself as a trusted advisor.
>
> Addresses Objections: Follow-up gives you an opportunity to address any objections or concerns that the prospect may have raised during the initial cold call.
> By providing additional information or clarification, you can alleviate their concerns and move the sales process forward.

Keeps You Top-of-Mind: Regular follow-up keeps you top-of-mind with prospects and ensures that they remember you when they're ready to make a decision.
By staying in touch consistently, you increase your chances of being chosen as the preferred vendor when the time comes.

Drives Action: Follow-up prompts prospects to take action and move forward in the sales process.
By providing clear next steps and deadlines, you create a sense of urgency and motivate prospects to make a decision.

Crafting Compelling Follow-Up Messages

Crafting compelling follow-up messages is essential for grabbing the prospect's attention and encouraging them to engage with you further.

Here are some tips for crafting effective follow-up messages:

Personalise Your Message: Personalization is key to effective follow-up. Reference specific details from your previous conversation, such as a pain point or challenge the prospect mentioned, to show that you're paying attention and listening to their needs.

Provide Value: Offer something of value in your follow-up message, such as a helpful resource, industry insight, or solution to a problem the prospect is facing.
By providing value upfront, you demonstrate your expertise and establish credibility.

Keep It Concise: Keep your follow-up message concise and to the point. Avoid overwhelming the prospect with too much information or lengthy paragraphs. Instead, focus on communicating your key points clearly and succinctly.

Include a Call to Action: Every follow-up message should include a clear call to action that prompts the prospect to take the next step.
Whether it's scheduling a follow-up call, requesting a demo, or downloading a resource, make it easy for the prospect to move forward.

Follow Up Multiple Times: Don't be discouraged if you don't hear back from the prospect after the first follow-up message.
Follow up multiple times at regular intervals to stay top-of-mind and increase your chances of getting a response.

Techniques for Staying Top-of-Mind

Staying top-of-mind with prospects is essential for maintaining their interest and keeping the sales process moving forward.

Here are some techniques for staying top-of-mind using the Straight Line Technique:

Send Personalised Emails: Send personalised emails to prospects that reference previous conversations and provide relevant information or resources.
Tailor your messaging to their specific needs and interests to grab their attention.

Connect on Social Media: Connect with prospects on social media platforms such as LinkedIn to stay in touch and engage with them on a more personal level.
Share valuable content, comment on their posts, and participate in relevant discussions to maintain visibility.

Send Thoughtful Gifts: Send thoughtful gifts or tokens of appreciation to prospects to show that you value their business and appreciate their time.
Personalise the gift based on their interests or preferences to make a lasting impression.

Offer Exclusive Insights: Share exclusive insights or industry trends with prospects to demonstrate your expertise and provide value.
Offer to set up a call to discuss how these insights relate to their business and how your solution can help address their challenges.

Leveraging the Straight Line Technique for Follow-Up

The Straight Line Technique provides a structured framework for follow-up that keeps prospects engaged and moves them closer to a positive decision.

Here's how you can leverage the Straight Line Technique for follow-up:

> Engage: Use engaging subject lines and opening statements to capture the prospect's attention and encourage them to open your follow-up message.
>
> Qualify: Qualify the prospect further by asking questions about their needs, challenges, and objectives in your follow-up message.
> Use their responses to tailor your messaging and provide relevant solutions.
>
> Present: Present the value and benefits of your offering in your follow-up message, reinforcing key points from your initial cold call and addressing any objections or concerns that were raised.
>
> Close: Close the follow-up message with a clear call to action that prompts the prospect to take the next step, such as scheduling a follow-up call or requesting more information.

Overcoming Common Challenges in Follow-Up

While follow-up is essential for maintaining momentum in the sales process, it can also present challenges.

Here are some common challenges and strategies for overcoming them:

> Lack of Response: If you don't receive a response to your follow-up message, don't give up.
> Follow up multiple times at regular intervals, and try different communication channels to increase your chances of converting the prospect into a sale.
>
> Timing Issues: Timing can be critical in follow-up. Avoid overwhelming the prospect with too many follow-up messages too quickly, but also be mindful of not waiting too long between communications. Find the right balance and timing that works best for your prospect and their buying cycle.
>
> Lack of Personalization: Generic follow-up messages are less likely to resonate with prospects.
> Take the time to personalise each follow-up message based on the prospect's specific needs, interests, and preferences.

Reference previous conversations and tailor your messaging accordingly to demonstrate that you're attentive to their individual situation.

Failure to Provide Value: Each follow-up message should provide some form of value to the prospect, whether it's helpful information, industry insights, or solutions to their challenges.
Avoid sending follow-up messages that are purely self-promotional or sales-focused.
Instead, focus on providing genuine value that demonstrates your expertise and builds trust with the prospect.

Conclusion

Effective follow-up is essential for maintaining momentum, building rapport, and ultimately converting prospects into customers.

By crafting compelling follow-up messages, staying top-of-mind with prospects, and leveraging the Straight Line Technique for follow-up, you can increase your chances of success and achieve better results in your cold calling efforts.

In the following chapters, we'll continue to explore advanced techniques and best practices for mastering the art of cold calling.

Chapter 14: Advanced Techniques for Experienced Cold Callers

Experienced cold callers understand that success in sales requires continuous learning, adaptation, and mastery of advanced techniques.

In this chapter, we'll delve into advanced strategies, tactics, and mindset shifts that can take your cold calling efforts to the next level and drive even greater results using the Straight Line Technique.

Elevating Your Cold Calling Game

As an experienced cold caller, you've likely mastered the basics of the Straight Line Technique and achieved a level of proficiency in connecting with prospects and closing deals.

Now it's time to elevate your game and unlock new levels of success by implementing advanced techniques and strategies. Here's how:

> Refine Your Pitch: Take a critical look at your pitch and identify areas for improvement.
> Refine your messaging, eliminate unnecessary details, and focus on communicating the most compelling aspects of your offering concisely.
>
> Master Objection Handling: Anticipate objections that prospects may raise during the sales process and prepare strategic responses in advance. Develop rebuttals that address objections effectively while reinforcing the value proposition of your product or service.
>
> Develop Your Unique Selling Proposition (USP): Identify and articulate what sets your offering apart from the competition.
> Develop a compelling USP that highlights the unique benefits and advantages of choosing your solution over alternatives.
>
> Expand Your Prospect Universe: Don't limit yourself to the same pool of prospects.
> Continuously seek out new opportunities and explore untapped markets to expand your prospect universe and increase your potential for success.

Leveraging Social Selling

Social selling has emerged as a powerful strategy for building relationships, establishing credibility, and generating leads in today's digital age.

Here are some advanced techniques for leveraging social selling in your cold calling efforts:

> Build a Strong Personal Brand: Invest time in cultivating a strong personal brand on social media platforms such as LinkedIn.
> Share valuable content, engage with industry influencers, and showcase your expertise to attract and engage prospects.

Utilise Advanced Search Filters: Leverage advanced search filters and Boolean operators to refine your search criteria and identify highly targeted prospects on social media.
Use keywords, company size, industry, and other parameters to narrow down your search results effectively.

Engage in Thought Leadership: Position yourself as a thought leader in your industry by sharing insights, best practices, and relevant content on social media.
Write articles, participate in group discussions, and offer valuable advice to demonstrate your expertise and credibility.

Leverage Social Listening: Monitor social media channels for mentions of your brand, industry trends, and relevant keywords using social listening tools.

Engage with prospects who are discussing topics related to your offering and provide helpful information or solutions to their challenges.

Implementing Account-Based Selling (ABS)

Account-based selling (ABS) is a strategic approach that focuses on targeting high-value accounts and customising outreach efforts to meet the specific needs of key decision-makers within those accounts.

Here's how to implement ABS effectively:

Identify Ideal Customer Profiles (ICPs): Define your ideal customer profiles based on criteria such as industry, company size, revenue, and strategic fit.

Use data analysis and market research to identify accounts that match your ICPs.

Build Target Account Lists: Create target account lists of high-potential prospects that align with your ICPs.
Prioritise accounts based on their potential value and likelihood of conversion.

Personalise Outreach Efforts: Tailor your outreach efforts to each target account and individual decision-maker within the organisation.
Craft personalised messages that address their specific pain points, challenges, and objectives.

Leverage Multi-Channel Engagement: Engage with prospects across multiple channels, including email, phone, social media, and in-person meetings.

Coordinate your outreach efforts to create a cohesive and personalised experience for each prospect.

Harnessing the Power of Data Analytics

Data analytics provides valuable insights into prospect behaviour, market trends, and sales performance, allowing you to make informed decisions and optimise your cold calling efforts.

Here's how to harness the power of data analytics:

Track Key Metrics: Monitor key performance indicators (KPIs) such as call-to-connect ratio, conversion rate, and average deal size to measure the effectiveness of your cold calling efforts.
Identify areas for improvement and adjust your strategy accordingly

Segment Your Audience: Segment your audience based on demographic, firmographic, and behavioural data to tailor your messaging and outreach efforts more effectively.
Customise your approach based on the unique needs and preferences of each segment.

Implement Predictive Analytics: Use predictive analytics to identify patterns and trends in prospect behaviour and predict future outcomes.
Leverage machine learning algorithms and predictive modelling techniques to anticipate customer needs and make proactive decisions.

Optimise Sales Processes: Analyse sales processes and workflows to identify bottlenecks, inefficiencies, and areas for optimization.

Use data-driven insights to streamline processes, improve productivity, and enhance the overall customer experience.

Conclusion

Mastering advanced techniques is essential for experienced cold callers looking to take their sales efforts to the next level and achieve greater success using the Straight Line Technique.

By refining your pitch, leveraging social selling, implementing account-based selling, and harnessing the power of data analytics, you can elevate your cold calling game and drive better results in your sales efforts.

In the following chapters, we'll continue to explore advanced strategies and best practices for mastering the art of cold calling.

Chapter 15: The Importance of Persistence and Resilience

Persistence and resilience are two essential qualities that separate successful cold callers from the rest.

In this chapter, we'll explore why these qualities are crucial for cold calling success, how to cultivate them, and practical strategies for maintaining motivation and overcoming obstacles using the Straight Line Technique.

Understanding Persistence and Resilience

Persistence is the ability to continue pursuing your goals despite facing challenges, setbacks, or rejection.

Resilience, on the other hand, is the ability to bounce back from adversity, adapt to change, and maintain a positive attitude in the face of obstacles.

Both qualities are essential for cold calling success because:

- Cold calling can be a tough and demanding endeavour, requiring perseverance and determination to push through rejection and maintain momentum.
- Resilience helps cold callers navigate the ups and downs of the sales process, bounce back from setbacks, and stay focused on their goals.

Cultivating Persistence and Resilience

While some people may naturally possess traits of persistence and resilience, these qualities can also be cultivated and developed over time.

Here are some strategies for cultivating persistence and resilience in your cold calling efforts:

> Set Clear Goals: Establish specific, measurable, and achievable goals for your cold calling activities.
> Break down large goals into smaller milestones and celebrate your progress along the way to stay motivated.
>
> Develop a Growth Mindset: Adopt a growth mindset that views challenges as opportunities for learning and growth rather than obstacles to success.
>
> Embrace failure as a natural part of the learning process and focus on what you can control.
>
> Stay Positive: Maintain a positive attitude and outlook, even in the face of rejection or adversity.
> Surround yourself with supportive colleagues, mentors, and resources that uplift and inspire you to keep going.
>
> Practice Self-Care: Take care of your physical, mental, and emotional well-being by prioritising self-care activities such as exercise, meditation, and hobbies.
> Set boundaries to prevent burnout and recharge your energy reserves regularly.
>
> Seek Feedback and Support: Solicit feedback from peers, mentors, and supervisors to identify areas for improvement and gain new perspectives on your cold calling efforts.
> Lean on your support network for encouragement and guidance during challenging times.

Strategies for Maintaining Motivation

Maintaining motivation is crucial for sustaining persistence and resilience in your cold calling efforts.

Here are some strategies for staying motivated and focused on your goals:

Visualise Success: Take time to visualise your goals and imagine yourself achieving them.
Create a vision board or mental imagery that represents your desired outcomes and revisit it regularly to stay motivated.

Celebrate Small Wins: Acknowledge and celebrate every small win and milestone you achieve in your cold calling efforts.
Whether it's securing a meeting with a prospect or overcoming an objection, celebrate your progress and use it as fuel to keep going.

Stay Connected to Your Why: Remind yourself of why you started cold calling in the first place and the larger purpose behind your efforts.
Whether it's achieving financial freedom, helping customers solve problems, or advancing in your career, stay connected to your why to stay motivated.

Find Inspiration: Surround yourself with sources of inspiration that motivate and energise you.
Read books, listen to podcasts, attend seminars, or connect with successful cold callers who inspire you to reach new heights in your own efforts.

Reward Yourself: Treat yourself to rewards and incentives for reaching specific milestones or achieving challenging goals.

Whether it's a small indulgence like a coffee or a more significant reward like a weekend getaway, use rewards to incentivize progress and maintain motivation.

Overcoming Obstacles with the Straight Line Technique

The Straight Line Technique provides a structured framework for overcoming obstacles and maintaining momentum in your cold calling efforts.

Here's how you can leverage the Straight Line Technique to cultivate persistence and resilience:

Engage: Use engaging opening statements and compelling hooks to capture the prospect's attention and overcome initial resistance.
Focus on building rapport and establishing trust to create a connection with the prospect from the outset.

Qualify: Qualify prospects effectively by asking probing questions and actively listening to their responses.
Identify their needs, challenges, and objectives to tailor your pitch and position your offering as the ideal solution.

Present: Present your offering in a clear, concise, and compelling manner that highlights its unique value and benefits.
Anticipate objections and address them proactively to alleviate any concerns the prospect may have.

Close: Close the deal confidently by using trial closes and assumptive language to move the prospect towards a positive decision.
Overcome objections with confidence and persistence, and ask for the sale directly to seal the deal.

Conclusion

Persistence and resilience are essential qualities for success in cold calling, enabling sales professionals to overcome obstacles, maintain motivation, and achieve their goals using the Straight Line Technique.

By cultivating these qualities, staying motivated, and leveraging the strategies outlined in this chapter, you can navigate the challenges of cold calling with confidence and achieve greater success in your sales efforts.

In the following chapters, we'll continue to explore advanced techniques and best practices for mastering the art of cold calling.

Chapter 16: Measuring Success: Metrics and Analytics

Measuring success is essential for evaluating the effectiveness of your cold calling efforts and identifying areas for improvement.

In this chapter, we'll explore the key metrics and analytics that you should track to gauge the performance of your cold calling campaigns using the Straight Line Technique

The Importance of Metrics and Analytics

Metrics and analytics provide valuable insights into various aspects of your cold calling efforts, including lead generation, prospect engagement, conversion rates, and overall sales performance.

By tracking and analysing relevant metrics, you can:

- Identify strengths and weaknesses in your cold calling strategy
- Measure the ROI of your sales and marketing initiatives
- Optimise your processes to increase efficiency and effectiveness
- Make data-driven decisions to improve results and drive better outcomes

Key Metrics for Cold Calling Success

Several key metrics are critical for measuring the success of your cold calling campaigns.

Here are some essential metrics to track:

> Call-to-Connect Ratio: The ratio of successful connections (e.g., conversations with prospects) to the total number of calls made.
> This metric measures the effectiveness of your cold calling efforts in reaching and engaging prospects.
>
> Conversion Rate: The percentage of prospects who take a desired action, such as scheduling a meeting, making a purchase, or signing up for a demo, out of the total number of prospects contacted.
> This metric measures the effectiveness of your sales pitch and closing techniques.

Average Deal Size: The average monetary value of a closed deal or sale. This metric provides insights into the value of your sales opportunities and helps forecast future revenue.

Sales Cycle Length: The average amount of time it takes to close a deal from initial contact to conversion. This metric measures the efficiency of your sales process and helps identify bottlenecks or delays that may impact sales velocity.

Lead Response Time: The average time it takes for your sales team to respond to inbound leads or inquiries.

This metric measures the speed and effectiveness of your lead follow-up efforts and can impact conversion rates.

Pipeline Velocity: The rate at which prospects move through your sales pipeline, from initial contact to conversion. This metric measures the efficiency of your sales pipeline and helps forecast future revenue.

Leveraging Analytics Tools

To effectively track and analyse key metrics, it's essential to leverage analytics tools and software solutions designed for sales and marketing professionals.

Here are some popular analytics tools used in cold calling:

CRM (Customer Relationship Management) Software: CRM software provides a centralised platform for managing customer data, tracking interactions, and monitoring the sales pipeline.
It offers reporting and analytics features that enable you to measure key metrics and generate insights into sales performance.

Call Tracking Software: Call tracking software allows you to monitor and analyse phone calls made by your sales team.
It provides insights into call volume, duration, and outcomes, helping you identify trends and patterns in prospect engagement.

Email Analytics Tools: Email analytics tools provide insights into email open rates, click-through rates, and engagement metrics.

They allow you to track the effectiveness of your email outreach efforts and optimise your campaigns for better results.

Sales Performance Dashboards: Sales performance dashboards offer real-time visibility into key metrics and KPIs, allowing you to monitor performance, identify trends, and make data-driven decisions.
They provide customizable reports and visualisations that make it easy to track progress and measure success.

Implementing Data-Driven Decision-Making

Data-driven decision-making is the process of using data and analytics to inform strategic and tactical decisions in your cold calling efforts.

Here are some best practices for implementing data-driven decision-making:

Define Clear Objectives: Start by defining clear objectives and goals for your cold calling campaigns. Identify the key metrics that align with your objectives and establish benchmarks for success.

Collect Relevant Data: Gather relevant data from multiple sources, including CRM systems, call tracking software, and email analytics tools.
Ensure that the data is accurate, complete, and up-to-date to provide meaningful insights.

Analyse Data Trends: Analyse data trends and patterns to identify correlations, anomalies, and opportunities for improvement.
Look for insights that can help optimise your cold calling strategy and drive better results.

Experiment and Iterate: Test different approaches, techniques, and strategies in your cold calling campaigns and measure their impact on key metrics. Iterate based on the results of your experiments and continuously refine your approach for better performance.

Monitor Performance Regularly: Monitor performance regularly and track progress towards your goals.

Use sales performance dashboards and reports to keep stakeholders informed and identify areas where intervention may be needed.

Case Study: Using Analytics to Optimise Cold Calling Campaigns

Let's explore a hypothetical case study to illustrate how analytics can be used to optimise cold calling campaigns:

Case Study: XYZ Corporation

XYZ Corporation, a B2B software company, was struggling to generate qualified leads and convert them into customers.

By implementing CRM software with built-in analytics capabilities, they were able to track key metrics such as call-to-connect ratio, conversion rate, and pipeline velocity.

By analysing the data collected from their cold calling campaigns, XYZ Corporation identified areas for improvement, including:

- Optimising their sales pitch and messaging to better resonate with their target audience
- Adjusting their lead qualification criteria to focus on higher-value opportunities
- Streamlining their sales process to reduce friction and accelerate deal velocity

As a result of these optimizations, XYZ Corporation saw a significant improvement in their cold calling performance, with an increase in conversion rates and a decrease in the sales cycle length.

By leveraging analytics to inform their decision-making, they were able to achieve better results and drive business growth.

Conclusion

Measuring success through metrics and analytics is essential for evaluating the effectiveness of your cold calling efforts and driving continuous improvement using the Straight Line Technique.

By tracking key metrics, leveraging analytics tools, implementing data-driven decision-making, and learning from case studies, you can optimise your cold calling campaigns and achieve better results.

In the following chapters, we'll continue to explore advanced techniques and best practices for mastering the art of cold calling.

Chapter 17: Case Studies: Real-Life Examples of Cold Call Conversions

Case studies provide valuable insights into real-life scenarios where the Straight Line Technique has been successfully applied to convert cold calls into customers.

In this chapter, we'll examine several case studies across different industries to illustrate the effectiveness of the Straight Line Technique and highlight key learnings for cold calling success.

Case Study 1: Software as a Service (SaaS) Company

Background: A SaaS company specialising in project management software targeted small to medium-sized businesses (SMBs) as their primary market.

Their sales team struggled to generate qualified leads and close deals through traditional prospecting methods.

Approach: The sales team adopted the Straight Line Technique to streamline their cold calling process and improve conversion rates.

They focused on engaging prospects with personalised opening statements, addressing objections effectively, and closing deals confidently using trial closes.

Results: By implementing the Straight Line Technique, the SaaS company saw a significant improvement in their cold calling performance.

They achieved a 30% increase in call-to-connect ratio, a 20% increase in conversion rate, and a 25% reduction in the sales cycle length. The sales team closed several high-value deals with SMBs, resulting in a substantial increase in revenue and market share.

Key Learnings:

- Personalization and relevance are critical for engaging prospects and capturing their attention during cold calls.
- Effective objection handling and trial closes can overcome scepticism and hesitation, leading to higher conversion rates.
- Confidence and conviction in your pitch are essential for building trust and credibility with prospects and closing deals successfully.

Case Study 2: Financial Services Firm

Background: A financial services firm specialising in retirement planning and wealth management targeted high-net-worth individuals (HNWIs) as their ideal clients.

Their sales team struggled to connect with busy professionals and convince them to schedule consultations.

Approach: The sales team adopted a consultative approach using the Straight Line Technique to position themselves as trusted advisors and provide personalised solutions tailored to each prospect's financial goals and objectives.

They leveraged data analytics and market insights to identify qualified leads and prioritise outreach efforts.

Results: By implementing the Straight Line Technique, the financial services firm achieved a 40% increase in appointment scheduling and a 25% increase in conversion rate.

They secured several high-value clients with significant assets under management (AUM), resulting in a substantial increase in revenue and profitability.

Key Learnings:

- Building rapport and establishing trust are essential for establishing credibility and fostering long-term relationships with high-net-worth clients.
- Providing personalised solutions and demonstrating expertise can differentiate you from competitors and position you as a trusted advisor.
- Leveraging data analytics and market insights can help identify high-value opportunities and prioritise outreach efforts effectively.

Case Study 3: Business Consulting Firm

Background: A business consulting firm specialising in strategy and operations targeted mid-sized enterprises across various industries.

Their sales team struggled to articulate the value proposition of their services and differentiate themselves from competitors.

Approach: The sales team adopted the Straight Line Technique to structure their cold calls effectively and communicate the unique benefits of their consulting services.

They focused on understanding prospect needs and challenges, demonstrating expertise through case studies and testimonials, and closing deals through value-based selling.

Results: By implementing the Straight Line Technique, the business consulting firm achieved a 35% increase in lead conversion rate and a 30% increase in average deal size.

They secured several high-profile clients and delivered measurable results in terms of revenue growth, cost savings, and operational efficiency improvements.

Key Learnings:

- Effective storytelling and evidence-based selling can provide tangible proof of the value proposition and credibility of your services.
- Demonstrating expertise through case studies, testimonials, and industry insights can build confidence and trust with prospects and facilitate decision-making.
- Focusing on value-based selling and aligning your solutions with prospect objectives can create win-win outcomes and drive better results.

Conclusion

These case studies highlight the effectiveness of the Straight Line Technique in converting cold calls into customers across different industries and target markets.

By adopting a structured approach, leveraging personalised messaging, and demonstrating expertise and credibility, sales professionals can overcome objections, build trust, and close deals successfully. In the following chapters, we'll continue to explore advanced techniques and best practices for mastering the art of cold calling.

Chapter 18: Conclusion: Mastering Cold Calling for Lasting Sales Success

In this final chapter, we'll bring together all the insights, strategies, techniques, and lessons learned throughout this book to provide a comprehensive overview of mastering cold calling using the Straight Line Technique. We'll recap key concepts, share actionable takeaways, and offer guidance on how to continue refining and optimising your cold calling efforts for lasting sales success.

Recap of Key Concepts

Let's start by summarising the key concepts and principles covered in this book:

Introduction to the Straight Line Technique: The Straight Line Technique is a structured approach to cold calling that involves guiding prospects through a series of stages—from engagement to closing—in a linear fashion.

Understanding the Psychology of Cold Calling: Successful cold calling requires a deep understanding of human psychology, including how to build rapport, establish trust, and overcome objections.

Setting Clear Objectives for Cold Calls: Clearly defined objectives are essential for guiding your cold calling efforts and measuring success. Whether it's scheduling appointments, generating leads, or closing deals, having clarity on your goals is critical.

Preparing Your Pitch: Research and Planning: Thorough research and strategic planning lay the foundation for effective cold calling.
By understanding your prospects' needs, challenges, and pain points, you can tailor your pitch to resonate with them and increase your chances of success.

Mastering the Opening: Hooking Your Prospect: The opening of your cold call sets the tone for the entire conversation. A compelling opening statement or hook can capture the prospect's attention and pique their interest, making them more receptive to your message.

Building Rapport and Establishing Trust: Building rapport and establishing trust are essential for fostering meaningful connections with prospects. Genuine empathy, active listening, and authenticity are key elements of rapport-building in cold calling.

Handling Objections with Confidence: Objections are a natural part of the sales process and provide opportunities for clarification and reassurance. By addressing objections confidently and empathetically, you can overcome scepticism and move the conversation forward.

The Art of Qualifying Leads: Qualifying leads effectively ensures that you're investing time and resources in prospects who are likely to convert into customers. Asking probing questions and actively listening to prospect responses are essential for lead qualification.

Presenting Your Solution Fffectively: Presenting your solution in a clear, concise, and compelling manner is crucial for persuading prospects to take action. Focus on highlighting the unique value and benefits of your offering and tailor your presentation to address prospect needs and preferences.

Overcoming Common Challenges in Cold Calling: Cold calling presents various challenges, including rejection, gatekeepers, and time constraints. By adopting a positive mindset, refining your approach, and continuously learning and adapting, you can overcome these challenges and succeed in cold calling.

Closing the Deal: Using the Straight Line Technique: Closing the deal is the culmination of your cold calling efforts.
By using trial closes, assumptive language, and confident closing techniques, you can guide prospects towards a positive decision and seal the deal effectively.

Follow-Up Strategies for Continued Engagement: Follow-up is essential for maintaining momentum and nurturing relationships with prospects.
By staying in touch, providing value-added content, and addressing any remaining concerns, you can increase your chances of conversion over time.

Leveraging Technology in Cold Calling: Technology plays a vital role in modern cold calling, from CRM systems and dialer software to email automation and social media platforms.
Leveraging technology effectively can streamline your processes, enhance productivity, and improve outcomes.

Advanced Techniques for Experienced Cold Callers: Experienced cold callers can take their skills to the next level by mastering advanced techniques such as social selling, account-based selling, and data analytics.
These techniques enable sales professionals to achieve greater success and drive better results in their cold calling efforts.

The Importance of Persistence and Resilience: Persistence and resilience are essential qualities for success in cold calling.

By cultivating these qualities and maintaining motivation, sales professionals can overcome obstacles, bounce back from setbacks, and achieve their goals using the Straight Line Technique.

Measuring Success: Metrics and Analytics: Measuring success through metrics and analytics provides valuable insights into the effectiveness of your cold calling efforts. By tracking key metrics, leveraging analytics tools, and implementing data-driven decision-making, you can optimise your cold calling campaigns and drive better results.

Case Studies: Real-Life Examples of Cold Call Conversions: Real-life case studies illustrate the practical application of the Straight Line Technique in converting cold calls into customers across different industries and target markets. These case studies provide valuable insights and best practices for achieving success in cold calling.

Actionable Takeaways

Now that we've recapped key concepts, let's distil actionable takeaways that you can implement in your cold calling efforts:

Set Clear Goals: Define clear objectives and goals for your cold calling campaigns to guide your efforts and measure success effectively.

Personalise Your Approach: Tailor your messaging and outreach efforts to each prospect's needs, preferences, and pain points to increase engagement and conversion rates.

Focus on Building Relationships: Prioritise building rapport, establishing trust, and nurturing relationships with prospects to foster long-term connections and drive repeat business.

Embrace Objections: View objections as opportunities for clarification and reassurance rather than barriers to success. Address objections confidently and empathetically to overcome scepticism and move the conversation forward.

Leverage Technology: Take advantage of technology tools and software solutions to streamline your cold calling processes, enhance productivity, and improve outcomes.

Cultivate Persistence and Resilience: Cultivate persistence and resilience to navigate the challenges of cold calling with confidence, bounce back from setbacks, and achieve your goals over the long term.

Guidance for Continued Growth

As you continue your journey of mastering cold calling using the Straight Line Technique, here are some guidance and best practices for continued growth and improvement:

Continuous Learning: Stay curious and committed to lifelong learning by seeking out new insights, techniques, and strategies for enhancing your cold calling skills.

Feedback and Reflection: Solicit feedback from peers, mentors, and supervisors to identify areas for improvement and reflect on your performance regularly.

Experimentation and Innovation: Be open to trying new approaches, experimenting with different techniques, and innovating in your cold calling efforts to stay ahead of the curve.

Adaptation to Change: Stay agile and adaptable in response to changes in the market, industry trends, and customer preferences.

Continuously evolve your approach to remain relevant and competitive in your cold calling efforts.

Networking and Collaboration: Build relationships with fellow cold callers, industry experts, and thought leaders to exchange ideas, share best practices, and collaborate on opportunities for growth and development.

Conclusion

Mastering cold calling using the Straight Line Technique is a journey that requires dedication, perseverance, and continuous improvement. By applying the insights, strategies, and techniques outlined in this book, you can enhance your cold calling skills, increase your effectiveness, and achieve lasting sales success.

Remember, success in cold calling is not just about closing deals—it's about building meaningful connections, delivering value to prospects, and creating win-win outcomes. Stay focused on providing exceptional service, solving problems for your customers, and making a positive impact in their lives.

As you embark on your cold calling journey, remember that every call is an opportunity to learn, grow, and make a difference. Keep
your eyes on the prize, stay persistent in the face of challenges, and remain resilient in pursuit of your goals. With dedication, hard work, and a commitment to excellence, you have the power to achieve extraordinary success in cold calling and beyond.

In closing, I'd like to express my sincere gratitude for embarking on this journey with me. Whether you're a seasoned sales professional looking to refine your skills or a newcomer eager to learn the ropes, I hope this book has provided you with valuable insights, actionable strategies, and inspiration to excel in your cold calling efforts.

Remember, mastering cold calling is not an overnight process—it takes time, effort, and perseverance. But with the right mindset, techniques, and support, you have everything you need to succeed.

As you continue your journey, I encourage you to stay curious, stay hungry, and never stop striving for greatness. The world of cold calling is full of opportunities waiting to be seized, and I have every confidence that you have what it takes to seize them.

Thank you for your time, your attention, and your commitment to excellence. Here's to your continued success in mastering cold calling using the Straight Line Technique.

Warm regards,

Jack Harmer

Thank you for reading "Cold Call Conversion: Mastering the Straight Line Technique." Be sure to check out my other book, "The Trust Factor: Mastering Authentic Sales Relationships," for further insights into building trust and authenticity in sales.

Your support means the world to me, and I hope these resources empower you to reach new heights in your sales career.

Happy selling!